6-3-67

*the Complete
Peddler's Pack*

by MAY JUSTUS

THE UNIVERSITY OF TENNESSEE PRESS   KNOXVILLE

illustrated by
JEAN TAMBURINE

the Complete
Peddler's Pack

games, songs, rhymes, and riddles from mountain folklore

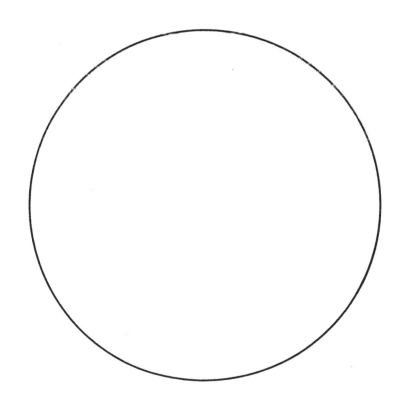

BOOKS BY MAY JUSTUS

THE COMPLETE PEDDLER'S PACK / A NEW HOME FOR BILLY
NEW BOY IN SCHOOL / SMOKY MOUNTAIN SAMPLER
WINDS A'BLOWING / BIG LOG MOUNTAIN / PEDDLER'S PACK
USE YOUR HEAD, HILDY / SURPRISE FOR PETER POCKET
CHILDREN OF THE GREAT SMOKY MOUNTAINS
LUCKY PENNY / LUCK FOR LITTLE LIHU / TOBY HAS A DOG
FIDDLERS' FAIR / HURRAH FOR JERRY JAKE / LIZZIE
BANJO BILLY AND MR. BONES / CABIN ON KETTLE CREEK
THE MAIL WAGON MYSTERY / MR. SONGCATCHER AND COMPANY
THE HOUSE IN NO-END HOLLOW / NEAR-SIDE-AND-FAR
THE OTHER SIDE OF THE MOUNTAIN / HONEY JANE
PETER POCKET'S BOOK /

"Beauty in the Lives of the Mountain Folk"

An Introduction by Edwin C. Kirkland

1411972

The Complete Peddler's Pack by May Justus has a rare distinction. The author is both the collector and the source of the material, and this gives a particular character to the book that is impossible for most of the other collections of folklore. It has an authenticity, a sincerity, and an air of being alive and present. Usually the collector or author of such publications goes to persons other than himself and records by various methods the songs, games, tales, and other types of folklore. The Great Smoky Mountains have long been a hunting ground for collectors, many of whom came from distant states. Their success has varied. A few sophisticated outlanders came convinced that the Southern mountaineer was a naïve being with queer ideas because he was so completely isolated from the outside world. The Southern mountaineer, very shrewd and quick to size up a stranger, would never be so impolite as to attempt to point out that the stranger was the one being naïve. Without batting an eye the mountaineer would proceed to assist the outlander in proving that the mountaineer was a queer creature, much queerer than the stranger had even suspected. Rather than tell a person he is a liar or is absurd, the mountaineer tells a bigger lie or absurdity; this traditional custom produced the tall tale, which is intended to fool no one, which takes a ready wit and skill, and which pleases everyone.

Most of the collectors who visited the Southern mountains, however, were wise enough to meet the people on a common level and to give evidence of a sincere interest in, and appreciation of, their ways and culture. Such were Mellinger E. Henry and Dorothy Scarborough. The people of the Southern mountains do nothing halfway. If they give their friendship and cooperation, they give one hundred percent, and much of their folk culture has been preserved because of their cooperation. Miss Justus, however, has the enviable position of being one of the people and thoroughly familiar with the folk culture which she is recording, so familiar in fact that practically all of it comes from her own memory, and has been in her memory so long that she does not recall from whom she learned many of the songs and games. No collector from the outside can record as accurately, or as fully, or as authentically as Miss Justus has done. Furthermore, she is proud of her culture, and rightfully so. I am reminded of another collector also proud of his culture, as the following titles demonstrate: *My Village Still Sings, Come to My Village,* and *My People Still Sing.* Miss Justus belongs to a community where the family is not scattered every evening because of different interests, but is unified by a common interest. Her father liked to fiddle, and her mother loved to sing. I am sure that friends and other relatives must have joined in as an integral part of the happy family group, and that the very young children learned the rhythm of the songs before they learned the words. Coming from this Anglo-Saxon and American culture, Miss Justus with her academic training at outstanding universities is qualified as few are to preserve in published form the cultural heritage of her people.

Francis B. Gummere said, "The great poems of the world are far greater than the greatest ballads; but no poet has ever had the power to compete with popular tradition on its own ground. Art can create far beyond the beauty of sea-shells, and on occasion can exactly reproduce them; but it cannot fashion or imitate their murmur of the sea" (Reed Smith, *South Carolina Ballads*, p. 8). As I examine the games, songs, rhymes, and riddles of *The Complete Peddler's Pack*, I realize that they are a part of the beauty of the Smoky Mountains along with the laurel and rhododendron of the spring and the gold and brown of the autumn leaves. And I wonder whether that beauty is as difficult to reproduce out of its natural habitat as is the murmur of the sea. Miss Justus has reproduced the natural habitat, as far as possible, in her short stories and novels, such as *Children of The Great Smoky Mountains*, *The House in No-end Hollow*, *Cabin on Kettle Creek*, and *Mr. Songcatcher and Company*. In these works Miss Justus's skill as a writer of fiction combines with her knowledge of the lore of her people to give a glimpse into the way folklore lives, grows, and is preserved in the rich heritage of the Smoky Mountains. Anyone who has read these novels for young folk and for those who love to be with young folk will, as he goes through *The Complete Peddler's Pack*, recreate in his imagination at least a part of the beauty in the lives of the mountain folk.

*for my father
who liked to fiddle
and my mother
who loved to sing*

the Complete Peddler's Pack

A Legacy of Folklore, page xi

Nonsense Rhymes

Pocket Full of Rocks, 2
Had a Little Mule, 2
Possum up a Gum Tree, 2
Warning to Book Thieves, 3
Indian Brew, 4
There Was an Old Woman, 5
Raccoon on a Rail, 5
I Know a Funny Thing, 6
Plow the Corn, 6
Spelling Rhyme, 6
Cake Recipe Rhyme, 7
Dolly Mariar, 8

Riddles, Tongue-Twisters, and Counting-Out Rhymes

Riddles, 10
Tongue-Twisters, 14
Counting-Out Rhymes, 15

Songs and Singing Games

Diller, Diller Dollar, 18
The Whistle Pig Song, 19
Sing a Little Hoe-Down Jordan, 20
Wishing Song, 23
Who Will Shoe My Little Feet, 24
What'll We Do with the Baby-O, 26
Old Farmer Grumble, 28
Dollar, Dollar, 31
Whoa, Mule Whoa, 32
Somebody Stole, 34
The Singing Bird, 36
Some Love Coffee, Some Love Tea, 38
Fiddler's Fair, 40
Tale of a Pig, 42
Bluebird, Blackbird, 44
Here Come the Dukes, 46
Among the Little White Daisies, 48
Sally Down Our Alley, 50
The Jolly Miller, 51
Go In and Out the Window, 52
Green Gravel, 54

Play-Party Games

Club Fist, 56
Whoopee-Hide, 58
I Count Ten, 59
Whistle and Find It, 60

Old Cat Tiggy, 60
Old Granny Hobble-Gobble, 61
Bogey Man Boo, 62
Witch Pot, 63
Rabbit in the Turnip Patch, 64
Slap Jack, 65
Jack in the Bush, 65
My Mother's Lost Her Thimble, 66
Chicken Thief, 67
Never Over, 67
Chickie, My Cranie-Crow, 68
Skipping Song, 69
Froggie in the Mill Pond, 70

Signs and Predictions

When Signs You See, 72
Weather Rhymes, 72
Witchwood, 75
Wish Rhyme, 76
Seven Little Blackbirds, 77
Spring Calendar, 78
Sneeze Rhyme, 80
Hearthfire, 81
Luck for Hallowe'en, 81
Dream Signs, 82

Index, 85

A Legacy of Folklore

As a child growing up in the shadow of the Great Smoky Mountains, I inherited most of the folklore treasure to be found in *The Complete Peddler's Pack*. The ballads, the play-party songs and games, the nonsense rhymes and riddles, I learned from my family, kinfolk, friends, and schoolmates.

My mother, from my earliest childhood recollection till a few years ago when she died at the age of eighty-six, sang from her rich memory the songs she had learned from her mother, who had come from England in 1835. My mother always sang best whenever she was busy about her household duties, indoors and out. She sang as she scrubbed clothes or churned. She sang to my father's fiddle as we sat about our fire at night. I listened and learned her songs without effort, hardly conscious of what I was learning.

The signs and predictions, the counting-out rhymes, the riddles and tongue-twisters were part of the common knowledge in our community. They were picked up here and there, passed along from one person to another. The nonsense rhymes were used mainly as recitations in school on Friday afternoons when all the pupils were expected to "say speeches." I never saw any of these in print till I used them in my own books.

In the yard of the old log schoolhouse where I went to school to my father, I first learned the fun of singing games. I cannot now recall any adult teaching us to play. No doubt the children taught one another. At any rate, I learned them so well, and loved so well what I learned, that I have been teaching these games ever since to children eager to play them as we did long ago.

After the lapse of so many years, it is quite impossible for me to recall the precise source of some items in this book. But I have, whenever I could do so, given credit to persons, schools, and localities where such credit is due.

To those of us who lived far removed from the stores and shops of a city, the visit of a peddler was a thrilling event. In his shoulder pack he carried many pretty and practical articles: bright ribbons, sweet-scented cakes of soap, neckties, needles, sewing thread, and dozens of other things. When the peddler loosened his load and spread its treasures on the floor, it was a sight to behold, one I can never forget. If the peddler's visit came at a time when we had not a penny to spend, he never begrudged us a glimpse of his wares, for he was a courteous man. From this long-ago memory came the suggestion that *Peddler's Pack* would be a very good title for a book that is a miscellany of fun and fancy belonging to the mountain region marked by the peddler's path.

May Justus

Tracy City, Tennessee
April, 1966

Nonsense Rhymes

Nobody, so far as I know, has a definite idea about the origin of these rhymes or knows who their authors may have been. Like many folk songs and fiddle tunes, they were known to some of my neighbors and kinfolk who could neither read nor write. They have been passed on by word of mouth from one generation to another. In my childhood these nonsense verses were often recited at school on the Friday afternoons when we had a special hour for "speeches." The older pupils usually gave serious and dignified recitations, mostly poems in their readers. But the little boys liked to get a laugh by rattling off one of those gems somebody at home had taught him for the occasion.

The following nonsense rhymes were given mostly as Friday afternoon recitations at Pig Trot School, near Bridgeport, Tennessee, during the years I attended, from 1905 to 1912.

Pocket Full of Rocks

With my pocket full of rocks,
  And my head full of knowledge,
I'd rather go to your school
  Than any other college.

Had a Little Mule

Had a little mule,
  And his name was Jack.
I rode on his tail
  To save his back.

Possum up a Gum Tree

Possum up a gum tree,
Rabbit in a hollow,
Skin the possum and rabbit, too,
For half-a-dollar.

Warning to Book Thieves

This warning, written on the flyleaf of
many schoolbooks, was taken from a copy
of *Lee's Third Reader*, 1907.

Don't steal this book, you wicked lad,
For (60) cents it cost my Dad.
And if you do, the Lord will know
And tell you to go down below.
But if this book should chance to roam,
Just box its ears and send it home!

Indian Brew

Old Doc Tucker from Yon Side was known as the Herb Man all over Cocke County, and even beyond in the early part of the century. He brewed his medicine from mountain herbs, put it into bottles, and sold it as a cure-all. His rawboned horse and ramshackle wagon were often seen in Newport, the county seat.

He would hitch in Courthouse Square and advertise his medicine by dancing around chanting this singsong while he waved a bottle about:

> Indian Brew—Indian Brew—
> Good for you and your family, too.
> There's hardly a pain that it won't stop;
> It's worth about a dollar a drop.
> Magic medicine, tried and true,
> Buy a bottle of Indian Brew!

4

There Was an Old Woman

There was an old woman
  Lived under a hill,
Put a mouse in a meal sack
  And took it to mill.
The miller he laughed
  And he teased the old wife:
"I never took toll
  Of a mouse in my life!"

Raccoon on a Rail

Raccoon a-sitting on the end of a rail,
Picking his teeth with the end of his tail.
Mulberry leaves and calico sleeves,
All schoolteachers are hard to please.

5

I Know a Funny Thing

I know a funny thing I want to tell:
Three little boys in a peanut shell.
One can read,
One can write,
One can smoke his grandpa's pipe.

Plow the Corn

Plow the corn,
Hoe the corn,
Listen for the dinner horn.
Hoe cake,
Ham meat,
Plenty good enough to eat.

Spelling Rhyme

H–u–huckle
B–u–buckle
H–u–huckle–y
H–u–huckle
B–u–buckle
Huckleberry pie.

Cake Recipe Rhyme

This is not really a nonsense rhyme, nor was it a school recitation. I learned it from my mother who used the recipe to make many a cake when I was a child. She baked it in layers that were put together with blackberry jam or apple butter—hence the name "stack cake."

> Three double-handsful and one
>   more of flour.
> Two cups of sweet milk, and one cup
>   of sour.
> A thumb pinch of soda, make no
>   mistake.
> And one cup of sorghum to make up
>   the cake.

Dolly Mariar

This singsong, known by many children in my childhood, was used sometimes as a chant in skipping rope. We often used wild grapevine.

Dolly Mariar jumped in the fire.
The fire was so hot,
She jumped in the pot.
The pot was so black,
She jumped in a crack.
The crack was so deep,
She jumped in the creek.
The creek was so shallow,
She jumped in the tallow.
The tallow was so soft,
She jumped in the loft.
The loft was so rotten,
She jumped in the cotton.
The cotton was so white,
She stayed there all night.

Riddles, Tongue-Twisters, and Counting-Out Rhymes

*These riddles, tongue-twisters, and counting-out rhymes
are derived from many sources. They are all part of
childhood knowledge and childhood fun.*

Riddles

What won't go up the chimney up,
But will go up the chimney down?
What won't go down the chimney up,
But will go down the chimney down?
(an umbrella)

Red in the valley,
Red on the hill.
Feed it, live it will.
Water it, it will die.
This is true, and not a lie.
(fire)

Crooked as a rainbow,
Teeth like a cat.
I bet a gold fiddle-stick
You can't guess that!
(a blackberry brier)

Thirty-two white calves
Standing in a stall—
Along comes a red cow
And licks them all.
(teeth and tongue)

Old or young,
It sticks out its tongue.
(a wagon)

10

Over the ground,
Under your nose,
It has as many heels as toes.
            (*a pair of shoes*)

Up and down the road it goes,
Or over fields instead.
Nothing of its body shows,
It travels on its head.
                (*shoe tack*)

Jigitty-jig, jigitty-jig—
What makes more fuss than a hungry pig?
Jigitty-jog, jigitty-jog—
What makes more fuss than a hungry hog?
                (*two hungry hogs*)

It never moves by day or night,
Yet keeps on going out of sight.
            (*a path or road*)

11

If you are wise, you can answer me—
How many sides are there to a tree?
　　　　(*two: outside and inside*)

This is as plain as the end of your nose—
The more you take from it, the bigger it grows.
　　　　　　(*a hole*)

High it flies,
Low it flies,
Yet has no wings
On which to rise.
　　(*smoke*)

What is it that sits upon a shelf,
And lives as long as it eats itself?
　　　　(*a candle*)

What happens in a minute,
Twice in a moment,
But not once in a thousand years?
(the letter "m")

Bridges great, bridges small—
This one is the least of all.
(the bridge of your nose)

Very nice, very neat—
Has teeth, cannot eat.
(a comb)

Anybody, if he will try
Can spell blind pig without an eye.
(p–g)

Although it never asked a thing
    Of any mortal man,
Everybody answers it
    As quickly as he can.
(a knock on the door)

Tongue-Twisters

How much wood would a woodchuck chuck
If a woodchuck would chuck wood?
He would chuck as much wood as a
    woodchuck would chuck,
If a woodchuck would chuck wood.

Said a flea to a fly in a flue:
Said the flea, "Oh, what shall we do?"
Said the fly, "Let us flee!"
Said the flea, "Let us fly!"
So they flew through a hole in the flue.

Sandy set a shady tree for Andy.

Pretty Little Polly Sane speaks a pretty little speech.

Counting-Out Rhymes

One little man a-driving cattle,
You can hear his money rattle.
How many pennies? One–two–three.
That's all—out goes he (or she).

I walked under an apple tree,
Down some apples fell on me.
One—two—three—four—
O–u–t goes out the door.

Three potatoes in a pot,
Take two out and leave one *hot*.
One for me, two for you,
And here's the hot potato, too!

Linnet, linnet, come this minute,
Here's a nest with goose eggs in it.
One for me, one for you,
One for the one who lost a shoe,
That's not me—it's y–o–u.

Who picked peppers,
Who picked a pocket?
Who stole my lady's locket?
Not you—not me—
This one—that one—
Count and *see!*

One, two, three, four,
Katie's at the kitchen door.
Five, six, seven, eight,
Eating cookies from a plate—
All that are left are my due.
That leaves none for y–o–u.

Songs and Singing Games

These songs and games were all well known in our part of Cocke County, Tennessee, when I was a child. I learned them at home, at school, and on the occasions when I visited kinfolk and neighbors.

Diller, Diller Dollar

This old chant was sung to tease anyone who might be
considered vain about his book-learning.

Dil-ler, dil-ler dol - lar; Dan-ny is a schol-ar!

Diller, diller dollar,
Danny is a scholar!
Now they say his head's too big
To poke it through his collar!

18

The Whistle Pig Song

(The whistle pig is a woodchuck or groundhog.)
This is an old fiddle tune. I first heard it played by my
father, Stephen Justus, in 1904–1905.

Come on, hur - ry and let's go — down,

Come on, hur - ry and let's go — down,

Let's catch a whis-tle pig in — the ground,

Come a ring - ding, din - gle - ing a di - de - oh!

Come on, hurry and let's go down,
Come on, hurry and let's go down,
Let's catch a whistle pig in the ground,
Come a ring-ding, dingle-ing a di-de-oh!

Up came Pappy from the plow,
Up came Pappy from the plow,
Catch that whistle pig, catch him now,
Come a ring-ding, dingle-ing a di-de-oh!

Up came Mammy from the spring,
Up came Mammy from the spring,
Whistle pig grease all over her chin,
Come a ring-ding, dingle-ing a di-de-oh!

19

Sing a
Little Hoe-Down Jordan

As I— was walk-ing— down the— road,

Sing a lit-tle hoe-down Jor-dan, I—

met a ter-ra-pin— and a toad, Oh, Je-ru-sa-

lem! And ev-'ry time the— toad would jump,

Sing a lit-tle hoe-down Jor-dan, The ter-ra-pin hid be-

hind a stump, Oh, Je-ru-sa-lem!

Chorus, after each verse

Shine on, shine on, Sing a lit-tle hoe-down Jor-dan

Shine on, shine on, Oh, Je-ru-sa-lem!

20

As I was walking down the road,
Sing a little hoe-down Jordan,
I met a terrapin and a toad,
    Oh, Jerusalem!
And ev'ry time the toad would jump,
Sing a little hoe-down Jordan,
The terrapin hid behind a stump,
    Oh, Jerusalem!

Chorus, after each verse
Shine on, shine on,
Sing a little hoe-down Jordan,
Shine on, shine on,
    Oh, Jerusalem!

As I was walking through the field,
Sing a little hoe-down Jordan,
A black snake bit me on the heel,
    Oh, Jerusalem!
I turned around to do my best,
Sing a little hoe-down Jordan,
And fell into a hornet's nest,
    Oh, Jerusalem!

21

A monkey dressed in soldiers' clothes,
Sing a little hoe-down Jordan,
Went out one day to shoot some crows,
    Oh, Jerusalem!
The crows they all did fly away,
Sing a little hoe-down Jordan,
The monkey will shoot another day,
    Oh, Jerusalem!

Old mister wood-pecker sittin' in a tree,
Sing a little hoe-down Jordan,
Fell in love with a pretty lady,
    Oh, Jerusalem!
She grew fickle and from him fled,
Sing a little hoe-down Jordan,
And ever since then, his head's been red,
    Oh, Jerusalem!

The chickens and the hens were goin' to roost,
Sing a little hoe-down Jordan,
When a hawk flew down and bit the old goose,
    Oh, Jerusalem!
She bit a little duck in the middle of the back,
Sing a little hoe-down Jordan,
Made the old duck go quack! quack! quack!
    Oh, Jerusalem!

Wishing Song

I wish I were an ap - ple, An
ap - ple on a tree; I'd hang so high no-
bo - dy Could climb up af - ter me.

I wish I were an apple,
   An apple on a tree;
I'd hang so high nobody
   Could climb up after me.

I wish I were a redbird,
   A redbird in a tree;
I'd fly so high nobody
   Could throw a rock at me.

I wish I were a squirrel,
   A squirrel in a tree;
I'd hide so quick no hunter
   Could take a shot at me.

I wish I were an angel
   Upon a Christmas tree;
I'd smile down on my darling,
   And he'd (she'd) smile up at me.

23

Who Will Shoe My Little Feet?

I remember this piece from the singing of my mother, Margaret Justus, who probably learned it from her mother, Sarah Brooks, over ninety years ago.

Oh, who will shoe my lit-tle feet, feet, feet? Oh,
who will shoe my lit-tle feet, feet, feet? Oh, —
who will shoe my lit-tle feet, When
I am in a dis-tant land?

Oh, who will shoe my little feet, feet, feet?
Oh, who will shoe my little feet, feet, feet?
Oh, who will shoe my little feet,
When I am in a distant land?

Oh, who will glove my little hands, hands, hands?
Oh, who will glove my little hands, hands, hands?
Oh, who will glove my little hands,
When I am in a distant land?

Oh, who will kiss my rosy lips, lips, lips?
Oh, who will kiss my rosy lips, lips, lips?
Oh, who will kiss my rosy lips,
When I am in a distant land?

What'll We Do with the Baby-O?

This old mountain lullaby should always be sung softly, and with a rhythm like that of a cradle rocking on the cabin floor. As I remember, my mother hummed the tune as the baby went to sleep toward the end of the song.

What-'ll we do with the ba - by - O?

What-'ll we do with the ba - by - O?

What-'ll we do with the ba - by - O? We'll

give it to it's mam - my - O.

1

What'll we do with the baby-O?
What'll we do with the baby-O?
What'll we do with the baby-O?
We'll give it to its mammy-O.

26

2

What'll we do with the baby-O? (*three times*)
We'll swing it high and swing it low.

3

What'll we do with the baby-O? (*three times*)
We'll rock it in its cradle-O.

4

What'll we do with the baby-O? (*three times*)
We'll dress it up in calico.

5

What'll we do with the baby-O? (*three times*)
We'll give it to its pappy O.

Old Farmer Grumble

This song was doubtless one that my grandmother learned in England before she came to Tennessee around 1835. My mother sang it with some variations of her own. This is the one I remember best.

There was an old man that lived in a wood, As you can plain-ly see,— Who said that he did more work in a day than his wife could do in three. "If this be true," the old wo-man said, "Why, this you must al - low,— That you shall do my work to - day, While I go drive the plow.—

There was an old man that lived in a wood,
   As you can plainly see,
Who said that he did more work in a day
   Than his wife could do in three.
"If this be true," the old woman said,
   "Why this you must allow,
That you shall do my work today,
   While I go drive the plow.

"Remember this is baking day,
   And you will have to make
A loaf of bread, an apple pie,
   A custard and a cake.
And you must wind the spool of thread
   That I spun yesterday,
And you must watch the speckled hen,
   For fear that she may stray.

"Be sure to milk the muley cow
   That she may not go dry,
And don't forget to feed the pigs
   That are within the sty."
The old man made the bread and pie,
   The custard and the cake,
But he forgot to make the fire,
   And so they did not bake.

The old man wound the spool of thread
   His wife spun yesterday,
But he forgot the speckled hen,
   And so she went astray.
The old man went to feed the pigs,
   The Mother Sow and ten,
But when he tried to fill the trough,
   He stumbled and fell in!

When by and by his wife came in,
   She found him in the bed,
But when he saw her, he sat up,
   And this is what he said:
"If I should live a hundred years,
   Why, still I should agree,
My wife does more work in a day
   Than I can do in three."

Dollar, Dollar

In this singing game the players are seated in a circle with one player, whose name is used in the song, standing in the center. Each one in the circle puts his left hand on his left knee, palm up. A player now holds a coin in his right hand and pretends to pass it to his right hand neighbor by patting his neighbor's left hand with his own right, then back to his own left. All players are patting, left and right, in time to the song, while the coin is slyly slipped around. When the center player thinks he has caught the one who has the coin, he taps his hand. If he guesses right, the one caught must take his place while the center player rejoins the ring.

Dol - lar, dol - lar, how it . wan - ders, from the right hand to the oth - er! Is it right, is it fair, to keep poor (Ma - ry) stan -ding there?

Dollar, dollar, how it wanders,
From the right hand to the other!
Is it right, is it fair,
To keep poor (Mary) standing there?

31

Whoa, Mule Whoa!

This is called a "fiddle-jig song" in the Smoky Mountains. My father played it, and my mother sang it in my early childhood.

Once I had an old gray mule, Old gray mule named Joe.

Repeat for Chorus

Took a week to go to mill __ 'Cause he was so slow.

Once I had an old gray mule,
    Old gray mule named Joe.
Took a week to go to mill—
    'Cause he was so slow.

Chorus, after each verse
Whoa back, whoa back, whoa back, Mule,
    Whoa back, Mule, I say!
Got no time to fool with you—
    Ride you anyway!

Swapped him for a frisky mule,
    Think his name was Ike.
Went so fast his feet caught fire
    Going down the pike.

Next I bought a mule named Ned—
　　Thought he had some sense.
Kicked his stable down one night,
　　And jumped a ten-rail fence!

Now I've got another mule—
　　Hasn't any name.
Hope he's better than the rest,
　　But I guess he's just the same!

Somebody Stole

This is another one of my father's "fiddle-jig songs."

Some-bo-dy stole my old coon dog, I wish they'd bring him back. He'd run the big pigs o-ver the fence, The lit-tle ones through a crack.

Somebody stole my old coon dog,
I wish they'd bring him back.
He'd run the big pigs over the fence,
The little ones through a crack.

Somebody stole my old brown mule,
  I hope he runs away.
I'll ride him clear to Tucker Town,
  And back again next day.

Somebody stole my old red hen,
  I wish they'd let her be.
She laid a good egg every day,
  On Sunday two or three.

Somebody stole my brindle cow—
  I hope she jumps the fence.
I wouldn't sell her for a dime,
  Or even thirty cents!

1411972

The Singing Bird

I saw a redbird in the air,
A redbird in a tree,
But a redbird in a bramble bush
Was the one that sang to me.

Chorus, after each verse
Birdie, birdie in the air
  Birdie in the tree!
But the birdie I like best of all
  Is the one that sings to me!

I saw a blackbird in the air,
  A blackbird in a tree,
But a blackbird in a berry bush
  Was the one that sang to me.

I saw a bluebird in the air,
  A bluebird in a tree,
But a bluebird in a lilac bush
  Was the one that sang to me.

Some Love Coffee, Some Love Tea

Some love_ cof - fee, some love_ tea,

Some love_ su - gar but they don't love me.

Some love coffee, some love tea,
Some love sugar but they don't love me.

Some love pudding, some love pie,
I love a boy (girl) with a bright blue eye.

Some love hoe cake, some love pone,
I love patty-cake and marrow bone.

Some love a riddle, some love a rhyme,
I love a sing-song any old time.

Some love the country, some love the town,
I love to journey up hill and down.

Some love the sunshine, some love dew,
I love you, honey, I love you!

Fiddler's Fair

This was once a singing game, but now it is used mostly as a two-part song for a boy and girl, who may sing it to the music of a guitar or banjo.

Oh, come with me to Fid-dler's Fair, To Fid-dler's Fair, to Fid-dler's Fair; Oh, come with me to Fid-dler's Fair, My hon-ey, oh, my hon-ey.

Boy: Oh, come with me to Fiddler's Fair,
To Fiddler's Fair, to Fiddler's Fair;
Oh, come with me to Fiddler's Fair,
My honey, oh, my honey.

Girl: How far is it to Fiddler's Fair,
To Fiddler's Fair, to Fiddler's Fair?
How far is it to Fiddler's Fair,
My honey, oh, my honey?

Boy: It's five long miles to Fiddler's Fair,
  To Fiddler's Fair, to Fiddler's Fair;
  It's five long miles to Fiddler's Fair,
   My honey, oh, my honey.

Girl: Too far to walk to Fiddler's Fair,
  To Fiddler's Fair, to Fiddler's Fair;
  Too far to walk to Fiddler's Fair,
   My honey, oh, my honey.

Boy: Then you may ride to Fiddler's Fair,
  To Fiddler's Fair, to Fiddler's Fair;
  Then you may ride to Fiddler's Fair,
   My honey, oh, my honey.

Girl: What shall we do at Fiddler's Fair,
  At Fiddler's Fair, at Fiddler's Fair?
  What shall we do at Fiddler's Fair,
   My honey, oh, my honey?

Boy: We'll dance and sing at Fiddler's Fair,
  At Fiddler's Fair, at Fiddler's Fair;
  We'll dance and sing at Fiddler's Fair,
   My honey, oh, my honey.

Girl: I'll go with you to Fiddler's Fair,
  To Fiddler's Fair, to Fiddler's Fair;
  I'll go with you to Fiddler's Fair,
   My honey, oh, my honey.

Tale of a Pig

In this song, the children join in the humming.

There was an old woman who had a little pig,
    Hm—m—m—m.
There was an old woman who had a little pig,
It wasn't too small and it wasn't too big.
    Hm——hm, hm!

The little old woman put piggie in a poke,
    Hm—m—m—m.
The little old woman put piggie in a poke,
And took it to mill to play a fine joke.
    Hm——hm, hm!

The little old woman put piggie in a pen,
    Hm—m—m—m.
The little old woman put piggie in a pen,
It never grew fat and it never grew thin.
    Hm——hm, hm!
The little old woman fed piggie in a pail,
    Hm—m—m—m.
The little old woman fed piggie in a pail,
And made a wee curl in the end of his tail.
    Hm——hm, hm!

The little old woman took piggie to the fair,
    Hm—m—m—m.
The little old woman took piggie to the fair,
The prettiest piggie of all the pigs there.
    Hm——hm, hm!

The little old woman came home from the fair,
    Hm—m—m—m.
The little old woman came home from the fair,
The pig had a bonny blue ribbon to wear.
    Hm—— hm, hm!

Bluebird, Blackbird

"Bluebird" is sung for a girl, "blackbird" for a boy.

All players except the "bluebird" (or "blackbird")
join hands in the circle and raise their arms to make
"windows."

In the first verse a boy or girl goes in and out of the
circle. On "I love you" he or she steps inside the circle
before a chosen partner. During the second verse this
partner is tapped on the shoulder three times by the
bluebird or blackbird. In the third verse the partners
dance around within the circle.

The first bluebird or blackbird rejoins the circle, and
the partner just chosen now starts the game again.

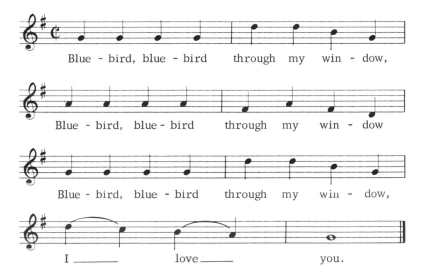

44

Bluebird, bluebird through my window,
Bluebird, bluebird through my window,
Bluebird, bluebird through my window,
    I love you.

Tap your true love on the shoulder (*three times*)
    I love you.

Come, let's dance around together (*three times*)
    I love you.

Here Come the Dukes

This is the first singing game that I remember playing at school—Bat Harbor School, which was taught by my father in 1904.

In this game there must be an equal number of girls and boys. The girls form a line facing the boys, several yards apart. The boys start the game by taking four steps forward and four steps back while singing the first verse. Then they stand still, facing the girls, as the girls reply with their verse, marching four steps toward the boys and back again. On the last verse each boy chooses his partner, and they walk, skip, or dance off, as they choose.

Here come the dukes a - rid - ing, A -
rid - ing, a - rid - ing. Here come the dukes a -
rid - ing, To the ran - some, hand - some tee.___

Boys: Here come the dukes a-riding,
A-riding, a-riding.
Here come the dukes a-riding,
To the ransome, handsome tee.

Girls: What will you have from us, Sirs,
From us, Sirs, from us, Sirs?
What will you have from us, Sirs,
To the ransome, handsome tee?

Boys: We seek a maid to marry,
To marry, to marry.
We seek a maid to marry,
To the ransome, handsome tee.

Girls: Will you have one of us, Sirs,
Of us, Sirs, of us, Sirs?
Will you have one of us, Sirs,
To the ransome, handsome tee?

Boys: You look too old and ugly,
And ugly, and ugly.
You look too old and ugly,
To the ransome, handsome tee.

Girls: We're quite as fair as you, Sirs,
As you, Sirs, as you, Sirs.
We're quite as fair as you, Sirs,
To the ransome, handsome tee.

Boys: The fairest one among you,
Among you, among you,
The fairest one among you,
I choose to go with me.

47

Among the Little White Daisies

Children join hands to form a ring, with one child in the center. Those in the circle sing the first and second verses, using actual names of the players. In the third verse the one in the center chooses a partner from the ring to join her. In fifth and sixth verses the center child makes-believe weeping sounds while partner "plays dead." On the last verse all children in the circle reach both hands out, and the center child taps hands and counts to twenty-four. The last child tapped must take center place, and the game continues.

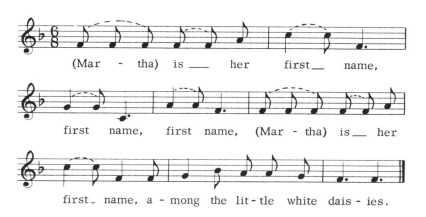

(Mar - tha) is ___ her first ___ name,
first name, first name, (Mar - tha) is ___ her
first ___ name, a - mong the lit - tle white dais - ies.

1

(Martha) is her first name, first name, first name.

(Martha) is her first name, among the little white daisies.

2

(Mason) is her last name, last name, last name.

(Mason) is her last name, among the little white daisies.

3

Choose partner

(Johnny) is his first name, first name, first name.

(Johnny) is his first name, among the little white
daisies.

4

(Johnson) is his last name, last name, last name.

(Johnson) is his last name, among the little white
daisies.

5

Weep and play dead

Now poor (Johnny) is dead and gone, dead and gone,
dead and gone.

Now poor (Johnny) is dead and gone, among the little
white daisies.

6

Left poor (Martha) a widow, a widow, a widow.

Left poor (Martha) a widow, among the little white
daisies.

7

Tap hands

Twenty-four children at her feet, at her feet, at her
feet.

Twenty-four children at her feet, among the little
white daisies.

Sally Down Our Alley

This group game for couples requires one extra girl. It is a fine game to play when a large number of boys and girls meet together—the larger the double circle, the better. The girls form an inner circle, and the boys, facing out, form an outer circle. The extra girl is "Sally," who skips around the "alley" or the space between the couples.

At the end of the verse, "Sally" stops beside the boy who happens to be nearest her. She places her left hand on his right shoulder, as he puts his right hand on her left shoulder. All couples do the same thing.

The verse is sung again as all the couples march to the right, and the girl who is left out becomes "Sally." Repeat to continue game.

The song has the same tune as *Ten Little Indians*.

> Here comes Sally down our alley,
> Here comes Sally down our alley,
> Here comes Sally down our alley—
> Who will she have for a partner?

The Jolly Miller

In this game each boy but one chooses his partner. The extra boy is the "jolly miller." He stands in the middle of the circle while the couples, arm in arm, march around him singing this song to the tune of *Turkey In The Straw*.

There was a jolly miller who lived by himself.
As the wheel went round, he made his wealth.
One hand in the hopper, the other in the bag,
As the wheel went round, he made his grab.

At the word "grab," all must change partners, and in this grand mixup, the jolly miller has a chance to get a partner for himself. The boy now left without a partner must be the jolly miller, and the game starts all over again.

Go In and
Out the Window

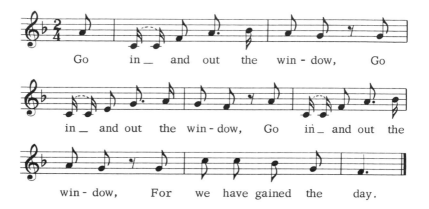

Go   in _ and out   the   win - dow,   Go
in _ and out   the win - dow,   Go   in _ and out   the
win - dow,   For   we   have gained   the   day.

In this game the boys and girls join hands forming a
circle and march around as they sing the first verse. One
player (a boy) passes in and out of the circle, as hands
lift high to let him "go in and out the window."

On second verse the circle stands still, and the single
player chooses another player to stand before while he
acts out the other verses. At the end of the fifth verse
another boy is chosen to be "It," and the game proceeds
as before.

1
Go in and out the window,
Go in and out the window,
Go in and out the window,
For we have gained the day.

2
Go forth and face your lover (*three times*)
For we have gained the day.

3
I kneel because I love you (*three times*)
For we have gained the day.

4
I measure my love to show you (*three times*)
For we have gained the day.

5
One kiss and then I leave you (*three times*)
For we have gained the day.

Green Gravel

This is a circle game for both girls and boys. All players, facing in, join hands and march around singing. Actual names of the players are used. A name is called in the song, and the one mentioned turns about and continues marching, facing out, still as a part of the circle. This game continues until all names are called and everyone faces outward.

Green gra-vel, green gra-vel! The grass is so green, The

fair-est young maid - en that ev - er was seen.

Green gravel, green gravel! The grass is so green,
The fairest young maiden that ever was seen.

Oh (Mary), Oh (Mary), your true love is dead.
He wrote you a message, so turn back your head.

He dressed you in scarlet, he dressed you in gold,
He dressed you in jewels all fine to behold.

Green gravel, green gravel! The grass is so green,
The fairest young maiden that ever was seen.

Play Party Games

Club Fist

This has always been a hearthside game in the Great Smoky Mountains, played by children on cold, shut-in days when they draw close to the great open fire for warmth and light and comfort.

The children sit down on the floor as a rule, with their knees close together. One child places his closed fist on his knee, thumb up. Another child catches this thumb in his fist, and so on till all players have stacked their fists up to the last.

The last child says to the owner of the fist just below his own:

Question: What have you got there?
  Reply: Club fist.
Question: Take it off—or knock it off?

Then the fist is either removed or "knocked off." This goes on until the last fist is reached, when the game takes this turn:

Question: What have you got there?
  Reply: A piece of bread and butter.

Question: Where's my share?
   Reply: The cat got it.

Question: Where's the cat?
   Reply: In the woods.

Question: Where's the woods?
   Reply: The fire burned it.

Question: Where's the fire?
   Reply: The water quenched it.

Question: Where's the water?
   Reply: The ox drank it.

Question: Where's the ox?
   Reply: The butcher killed it.

Question: Where's the butcher?
   Reply: The rope hung him.

Question: Where's the rope?
   Reply: The knife cut it.

Question: Where's the knife?
   Reply: The hammer broke it.

Question: Where's the hammer?
   Reply: Behind the door cracking hickory nuts,
       and the first one who laughs or shows his
       teeth will get a box with five nails (a slap).

The fun, of course, is to see who can hold out longest and keep from laughing.

Whoopee-Hide

This is the first outdoor group game that I can remember playing. The children in our family played it at home, at school, and whenever we went visiting. There are several variants of this game, but this is the version we played.

Any number can play. One is chosen as "It," and a home goal is chosen. Ours was usually the chimney corner or an apple tree.

"It" closes his eyes and counts while the others are hiding. He keeps counting till he reaches 100—or any number agreed upon. After reaching this. number, "It" calls out in a loud voice:

> Bushel of wheat,
> Bushel of rye!
> All who are are not ready,
> Holler, "I"!

If anyone calls out "I," "It" waits a few minutes longer, then calls:

> Bushel of wheat,
> Bushel of clover,
> All not hid
> Can't hide over.

Then he adds "Here I come," and starts out to hunt. As soon as he discovers a hidden player, he taps him if possible. If the player can beat "It" to the home goal, he goes free. The last player caught is "It" for the new game.

I Count Ten

This is one of the most popular hide-and-seek games and is suitable for playing outdoors, where the players can find many good hiding places in a hurry.

The one who is "It" shuts his eyes and starts counting loudly enough for all to hear him:

> One—two, I'll catch you,
> Three—four, and some more,
> Five—six, crooked sticks,
> Seven—eight, dinner's late,
> Nine—ten, pigs in a pen.

As soon as "It" says "pen," all of the other players must be safely hidden, or those still in sight must stand perfectly still where they are. Anyone caught moving has to come back to the starting place and count with "It"; both then start out to find the hidden players. The first one caught joins the hunters, and so on till all are found. Then the game begins again, with the first caught being "It."

Whistle and Find It

The players choose something to be hidden—a key, a knife, or another bright object. Then all of the players except one leave the room or a chosen part of the playground. The one left behind is "It," and he hides the object. He announces that it is hidden by whistling a familiar tune; the others then rush in, and the hunt begins. "It" guides the other players by whistling loudly when someone gets near the hiding place. The person who finds the object wins the game and is "It" the next time.

Old Cat Tiggy

The players in this game gather in a group outdoors, and one is picked to be the "cat." All the others are "mice." The mice are safe as long as they touch some piece of wood, even if it is a chip or a twig. The mice change places with one another, calling out as they run:

> Rag-a-rag, riggy,
> Old cat Tiggy!

The cat has to touch them before they find a safe place —some piece of wood to stand on or touch. All the mice caught have to take a turn at being the cat.

Old Granny
Hobble-Gobble

All of the players sit in a circle, except the one who is "It." This player stands in the center and selects a child to visit. "It" goes up to him and says: "Old Granny Hobble-Gobble sent me to you."

The child replies: "What for to do?"

"It" says, demonstrating the suitable motion: "Pat one foot just as I do."

Any action, such as "shake your head," "make a face," "dance around," may be specified by "It." The whole circle then follows suit, making the same actions.

Next, the one who has been visited must take the place of "It" and select another child to visit. This continues until all have taken turns.

Bogey Man Boo

In this game five, six, or a dozen players may have fun. One is the "bogey man," one is the "mother," the rest are her children.

The bogey man hides out of sight. The children sit in a row. The mother goes down the line, pointing to each child as she chants:

> I must go to the grocery store,
> Stay at home and bar the door;
> Be as quiet as you can,
> And look out for the Bogey Man.

Now the mother goes away and shuts her eyes so that she may not see what happens.

The bogey man comes in with a "Boo!" takes a child and hides it. This he does in turn till all are hidden away, and the bogey man sings out the signal for the mother:

> Bogey Man Boo
> Is ready for you!

Now the mother must hunt up all the children; each one, as he is found, joins in the search. When the last child is found, they all chase the bogey man. The one who catches him takes his place.

Witch Pot

One child is chosen for the witch. All of the other children choose some tree or post for home, where they are "safe."

The witch makes circles in the ground, one for each player. These are called "witch pots."

The children run out from their homes and dare the witch to catch them. When she catches one, she puts him into one of the witch pots that she guards. A prisoner in a pot can be freed by anyone who can reach him and touch him in spite of the witch. Of course he runs the danger of being caught himself and put in a pot.

Rabbit in the Turnip Patch

One player is the rabbit; another is the farmer. (After we had read the story of *Peter Rabbit,* we called the farmer Mr. McGregor.) All of the other players form a big circle. Inside the circle is the "turnip patch."

The rabbit slips inside the circle and begins hopping around, hunting for turnip greens. The farmer, who is outside, looks over the wall (the circle of players), and says, "I see a rabbit in my turnip patch. I'm going after him." Now the rabbit runs outside the circle, with the farmer in hot pursuit. In and out of the circle they go until the farmer catches the rabbit or until the rabbit saves himself by going around the full circle of players uncaught.

Slap Jack

In this game the children join hands, leaving one child to be "It." This player stands on the outside of the circle. The game begins by "It" going around and tagging someone on the shoulder. This player must leave his place at once, and run around the outside of the circle in the opposite direction from "It." The runner who reaches the vacant place first wins. The other becomes "It."

Jack in the Bush

Only two players are needed for this game. Each one must have an equal number of nuts or marbles or some other small things. A dozen is a good number to have on hand.

First player: Jack in the bush!
Second player: Cut him down.
First player (holding out a hand closed around any number of nuts he wants) : How many licks?

The second player guesses the number.

First player shows how many he has in his hand, and the second player must give him the number of nuts that will make up the difference, if any. This goes on until one player wins the game by having *all* the nuts in his possession.

My Mother's Lost
Her Thimble

This game is better for a large rather than small number of children, but ten or twelve in a circle are enough to have a lot of fun.

All the players except one stand in a ring, each holding the right wrist of the child on his left. This means that every person's right hand hangs free. Each player in the circle, in turn, passing a thimble or pretending to pass it, puts his free right hand over the hand of the one to the right of him, then over to the one to the left, saying:

> My Mother's lost her thimble
> I don't know where.
> It may be over here,
> It may be over there.

The extra player, "It," stands in the center of the circle and does his best to guess who holds the hidden thimble as it goes around. When "It" thinks he knows who has the thimble, he goes up to that player and taps his hand, saying: "Do you have it?"

If the guess is right, these two change places. If the guess is wrong, the center players must keep on guessing.

Chicken Thief

One player is the "fox" or "possum"; the rest are "chickens." These players must stay in some part of the playground chosen as a chicken yard. The chicken thief has a place called his den.

The game begins when the chicken thief comes out of his den and goes to the chicken yard to steal a chicken. He walks around the yard three times while all the chickens cackle or crow in alarm. At the end of the third round the thief tries to catch a chicken by tagging him on the shoulder three times. The tagged or "stolen" chicken then must go with the chicken thief and help him catch the other chickens.

Never Over

A player draws a circle on the ground, big enough for all players to have room to stand around it.

Next, a smaller circle is drawn inside, leaving a road or track between the two circles.

Two players take their places alongside each other in the track. Facing the same way, each puts a marble (or nut) on the ground and starts it around the track by flipping it with his fingers. If the marble goes outside the lines of the track, it is out for good, and the other player gets to choose a new opponent. The game is won by the player who manages to get his marble completely around the track first.

Chickie, My Cranie-Crow

For this game you must have an "old witch," a "mother hen," and as many "chickens" as possible.

The home of the old witch and that of the chickens are about twelve feet apart, with a line for the boundary.

The old witch stands outside the chicken pen and pretends to be looking for something on the ground.

The mother hen (with chickens behind her) chants:

> Chickie, my chickie, my cranie-crow,
> I went to the well to wash my toe.
> When I got back one chicken was gone.
> What time of day, Old Witch?
>
> *Old Witch:* One o'clock.

The chant and answer are repeated till the old witch answers (without warning) "Twelve o'clock." Then the witch tries to snatch a chicken. If she touches one and taps it three times, it must hop on one leg back home with the witch and stay there till she catches all the others—or has tried till she gives up.

Skipping Song

Right foot, left foot
  Any foot'll do!
Sugar foot has lost the bow
  From her little shoe!

Right foot, left foot,
  Any foot at all!
Sugar foot has lost her shoe
  Dancing at the ball!

Right foot, left foot,
  Any foot'll do!
Sugar foot has gone to seek
  For her little shoe!

Right foot, left foot,
  Any foot at all!
Sugar foot has found her shoe,
  Now she's lost her shawl!

Right foot, left foot,
  Any foot'll do!
Sugar foot has lost her shoe
  And her kerchief, too!

Right foot, left foot,
  Any foot at all!
Sugar foot has found them both,
  And hung them on the wall!

This is chanted, singsong fashion, in time to skipping
feet.

Froggie in the Mill Pond

Children join hands and form a circle around the one chosen to be the "frog," who stands in the center.

The children chant this rhyme as they march around the frog.

> Froggie in the mill pond,
>   Can't get him out;
> Take a little punch at him,
>   And make him turn about.

Circle now stops.

Someone behind the frog reaches in and taps him, then rushes back into circle and quickly squats as the frog tries to catch him. No one can be caught while squatting, but anyone on his feet, or even bent over, is fair game. If caught, the player becomes a frog and must go into the mill pond to help catch others.

Signs and Predictions

I learned these signs and predictions in my early childhood as they were quoted by members of my family and folks in our community, near Bridgeport, Tennessee, in Cocke County. At that time such signs and predictions were taken rather seriously.

I have included in this collection three poems of my own composition presenting various bits of folklore. These are signed personally.

When Signs You See

When signs you see,
   Attentive be.
When signs you hear,
   Then lend an ear.

Weather Rhymes

Between twelve o'clock and two,
You'll see what the day will do.

     Rain before seven,
     Quit before eleven.

When the wind's against the sun,
Trust it not, for back 'twill run.

When the smoke bites the ground,
Bad weather will be found.

Hoar frost on mornings twain,
On the third look for rain.

When the wind is in the north,
Man nor beast should venture forth.
When the wind is in the east,
It's good for neither man nor beast.
When the wind is in the west,
This for man and beast is best.

If the moon changes on Sunday,
Weather change is sure on Monday.

Onion skin very thin,
Pretty winter coming in.
Onion skin thick and tough,
Winter mighty cold and rough.

When April blows his horn (*thunder*)
It's good for hay and corn.

Mist in May,
Sun in June,
Makes the harvest ripen soon.

Change not a clout (*winter garment*)
Till May be out.

If the oak is out
Before the ash,
There'll be a summer
Of wet and splash.

If a cow beast scratch her ear,
Stormy weather's very near.

Witchwood

"Never burn witchwood," my old Granny said.
"If you do, bad luck will fall upon your head."

"Witchwood?" I cried, "What a funny name!"
"Sassafras," Granny said, "they are all the same."

We were digging roots for sassafras tea,
"What makes it witchwood? I don't see."

"Oh," laughed Granny, "it's an old-time trick—
A witch makes her broom from a sassafras stick."

M. J.

Wish Rhyme

Violets in the hollow,
  Poke greens in the dish,
Bluebird, fly up, fly up,
  Give me what I wish.

Cornstalks in the meadow,
  Pumpkins in the dish,
Brown bird, fly up, fly up,
  Give me what I wish.

Ice along the creek bank,
  Possum in the dish,
Snowbird, fly up, fly up,
  Give me what I wish.

Seven Little Blackbirds

Seven little blackbirds in a tree.
Count and you will fortune see.
One, you'll be sorry.
Two, you'll be glad.
Three, you will see a girl.
Four, a lad.
Five means silver.
Six means gold.
Seven means a secret that's never been told.

Spring Calendar

Treetops leafing early
  Over Little Twin;
Fiddle fern tips curly
  Up in Glowrie Glen.
Down in Darksome Hollow
  Dogwood's starry light;
Spring has come to follow
  Winter out o' sight.

Dandelions growing
  All along the creek,
Poke shoots will be showing
  In another week.
Hoe cake on the griddle,
  Sallet in the pot.
Answer me this riddle:
  Is it spring or not?

New ground patches ready—
    Break the rocky rows!
Hold the plowshare steady,
    Hurry up the hoes!
Whippoorwills a-warning
    Folks on Little Twin
"Plant your corn this morning,
    Springtime's here again!"

M. J.

Sneeze Rhyme

Sneeze on Monday,
  Sneeze for danger.
Sneeze on Tuesday,
  See a stranger.
Sneeze on Wednesday,
  Get a letter.
Sneeze on Thursday,
  Something better.
Sneeze on Friday,
  Sneeze for sorrow.
Sneeze on Saturday,
  Glad tomorrow.
Sneeze on Sunday,
  Happy Monday.

Hearthfire

Oak and hickory, green or dry,
Are the best of wood you can buy.
One is lasty, t'other's hot,
To bake the bread and boil the pot.

Luck for Hallowe'en

It was a wise old woman
　　Who gave this charm to me.
It works best on Hallowe'en—
　　Or so said she!

"Find a four-leaf clover,
　　Wear it in your shoe,
Right foot, left foot,
　　Either one will do.
It will lead you into luck
　　Before the day is through."

So find a four-leaf clover,
　　And put it to the test.
It *might* work any time—
　　But Hallowe'en is best.

M. J.

Dream Signs

To dream of fruit out of season,
Means trouble out of reason.

A snake in your sleep,
Means sorrow will creep.

To dream of a bird,
Is a secret heard.

When you dream of a stranger,
Look out for danger.

To dream of a letter,
Luck will be better.

If you dream of new shoes,
You will hear good news.

Dream of money,
Fortune sunny.

To dream of rain,
Means grief and pain.

To dream of snow,
Means bitter woe.

To dream of sun,
Means joy begun.

Would you have a dream come true,
Tell to one, but never two.

Lest a bad dream bring you harm,
Shake your pillow for a charm.

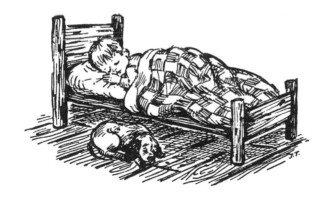

Index of Titles and First Lines

Although it never asked a thing, 13
Among the Little White Daisies, 48
Anybody, if he will try, 13
As I was walking down the road, 21

Between twelve o'clock and two, 72
Bluebird, Blackbird, 44
Bluebird, bluebird through my window, 45
Bogey Man Boo, 62
Bridges great, bridges small, 13
Bushel of wheat, 58

Cake Recipe Rhyme, 7
Change not a clout, 74
Chicken Thief, 67
Chickie, My Cranie-Crow, 68
Club Fist, 56
Come on, hurry and let's go down, 19
Counting-Out Rhymes, 15
Crooked as a rainbow, 10

Diller, Diller Dollar, 18
Dollar, Dollar, 31
Dolly Mariar, 8
Don't steal this book, you wicked lad, 3
Dream Signs, 82

Fiddler's Fair, 40
Froggie in the Mill Pond, 70

Go In and Out the Window, 52
Green Gravel, 54

Had a Little Mule, 2
Hearthfire, 81
Here Come the Dukes, 46
Here comes Sally down our alley, 50
High it flies, 12
Hoar frost on mornings twain, 73
How much wood would a woodchuck chuck, 14
H-u-huckle, 6

I Count Ten, 59
I Know a Funny Thing, 6
I must go to the grocery store, 62
I saw a redbird in the air, 36
I walked under an apple tree, 15
I wish I were an apple, 23
If a cow beast scratch her ear, 74
If the moon changes on Sunday, 73
If the oak is out, 74
If you are wise, you can answer me, 12
Indian Brew, 4
It never moves by day or night, 11
It was a wise old woman, 81

Jack in the Bush, 65
Jigitty-jig, jigitty-jig, 11
Jolly Miller, 51

Linnet, linnet, come this minute, 15
Luck for Hallowe'en, 81

Martha is her first name, first name, first name, 48
Mist in May, 74
My Mother's Lost Her Thimble, 66

Never burn witchwood, my old
    Granny said, 75
Never Over, 67

Oak and hickory, green or dry, 81
Old Cat Tiggy, 60
Old Farmer Grumble, 28
Old Granny Hobble-Gobble, 61
Old or young, 10
Once I had an old gray mule, 32
One little man a-driving cattle, 15
One-two, I'll catch you, 59
One, two, three, four, 16
Onion skin very thin, 73
Over the ground, 11

Plow the Corn, 6
Pocket Full of Rocks, 2
Possum up a Gum Tree, 2
Pretty Little Polly Sane speaks a
    pretty little speech, 14

Question: What have you got there,
    56

Rabbit in the Turnip Patch, 64
Raccoon on a Rail, 5
Rag-a-rag, riggy, 60
Rain before seven, 72
Red in the valley, 10
Riddles, 10
Right foot, left foot, 69

Said a flea to a fly in a flue, 14
Sally Down Our Alley, 50
Sandy set a shady tree for Andy, 14
Seven Little Blackbirds, 77
Sing a Little Hoe-Down Jordan, 20
Singing Bird, 36
Skipping Song, 69
Slap Jack, 65
Sneeze Rhyme, 80

Some Love Coffee, Some Love Tea,
    38
Somebody Stole, 34
Spelling Rhyme, 6
Spring Calendar, 78

Tale of a Pig, 42
There was a jolly miller who lived
    by himself, 51
There was an old man that lived in
    a wood, 29
There Was an Old Woman, 5
There was an old woman who had
    a little pig, 42
Thirty-two white calves, 10
This is as plain as the end of your
    nose, 12
Three double-handsful and one, 7
Three potatoes in a pot, 15
To dream of fruit out of season, 82
Tongue-Twisters, 14
Treetops leafing early, 78

Up and down the road it goes, 11

Very nice, very neat, 13
Violets in the hollow, 76

Warning to Book Thieves, 3
Weather Rhymes, 72
What happens in a minute, 13
What is it that sits upon a shelf, 12
What'll We Do with the Baby-O, 26
What won't go up the chimney up,
    10
When April blows his horn, 74
When Signs You See, 72
When the smoke bites the ground,
    72
When the wind is in the north, 73
When the wind's against the sun, 72
Whistle and Find It, 60
Whistle Pig Song, 19

86

Who picked peppers, 16
Who Will Shoe My Little Feet, 24
Whoa, Mule Whoa, 32
Whoopee-Hide, 58
Wish Rhyme, 76

Wishing Song, 23
Witch Pot, 63
Witchwood, 75
With my pocket full of rocks, 2